We Can Work It Out

Resolving Conflicts
Peacefully and Powerfully

*A presentation of Nonviolent
Communication™ ideas and their use by*

Marshall B. Rosenberg, Ph.D.

PuddleDancer
P R E S S

2240 Encinitas Blvd., Ste. D-911, Encinitas, CA 92024
email@PuddleDancer.com • www.PuddleDancer.com

For additional information:
Center for Nonviolent Communication
5600 San Francisco Rd., NE, Suite A, Albuquerque, NM 87109
Ph: 505-244-4041 • Fax: 505-247-0414 • Email: cnvc@cnvc.org • Website: www.cnvc.org

We Can Work It Out:
Resolving Conflicts Peacefully and Powerfully

© 2005 PuddleDancer Press
A PuddleDancer Press Book

PuddleDancer Press, Permissions Dept.
2240 Encinitas Blvd., Ste. D-911, Encinitas, CA 92024
Tel: 760-652-5754 Fax: 760-274-6400
www.NonviolentCommunication.com Email@PuddleDancer.com

Ordering Information
Please contact Independent Publishers Group, Tel: 312-337-0747;
Fax: 312-337-5985; Email: frontdesk@ipgbook.com or visit
www.IPGbook.com for other contact information and details about
ordering online

Author: Marshall B. Rosenberg, Ph.D.
Editor: Graham Van Dixhorn, Write to Your Market, Inc.,
        www.writetoyourmarket.com
Cover and Interior Design: Lightbourne, Inc., www.lightbourne.com

Manufactured in the United States of America

6th Printing, 2015

10 9 8 7 6

ISBN: 978-1-892005-12-0

Contents

We Can *Work It Out*

Introduction

For more than forty years, I've mediated in a wide variety of conflicts between parents and children, husbands and wives, management and workers, Palestinians and Israelis, Serbians and Croatians, and warring groups in Sierra Leone, Nigeria, Burundi, Sri Lanka, and Rwanda. What I've learned from dealing with conflicts at all these levels is that it is possible to resolve conflicts peacefully and to everyone's satisfaction. The likelihood of conflicts being resolved in this fulfilling way is significantly increased if a certain quality of human connection can be established between the conflicting parties.

I've developed a process called Nonviolent Communication™, which consists of thought and communication skills that empower us to connect compassionately with others and ourselves. My colleagues and I are extremely pleased with the many different ways that people are using Nonviolent Communication in their personal lives, work settings, and political activities.

In the following pages, I'll be describing how the process of Nonviolent Communication supports efforts to resolve conflicts peacefully. The process can be used either when we ourselves are directly involved in conflict, or when we are mediating the conflicts of others.

When I am called into a conflict resolution, I begin by guiding the participants to a caring and respectful quality of connection among themselves. Only after this connection is present do I engage them in a search for strategies to resolve the conflict. At that time we do not look for *compromise*; rather, we seek to resolve the conflict to everyone's complete satisfaction. To practice this process of conflict resolution, we must completely abandon the goal *of getting people to do what we want*. Instead, we focus on creating the conditions whereby *everyone's needs will be met*.

To further clarify this difference in focus (between getting what we want and getting what everyone wants), let's imagine that someone is behaving in a way that's not fulfilling a need of ours and we make a request that the person behave differently. In my experience, that person will resist what we request if they see us as only interested in getting our own needs met, and if they don't trust that we are equally concerned with meeting *their* needs. Genuine cooperation is inspired when participants trust that their own needs and values will be respectfully addressed. The Nonviolent Communication process is based on respectful practices that foster genuine cooperation.

Using Nonviolent Communication to Resolve Conflicts

The Nonviolent Communication practices that support conflict resolution involve:

a) expressing our own needs;

b) sensing the needs of others regardless of how others are expressing themselves;

c) checking to see if needs are accurately being received;

d) providing the empathy people need in order to hear the needs of others; and

e) translating proposed solutions or strategies into positive action language.

Defining and Expressing Needs (Needs Are Not Strategies)

It has been my experience that if we keep our focus on needs, our conflicts tend toward a mutually satisfactory resolution. Keeping our focus on needs, we express our own needs, clearly understand the needs of others, and avoid any language that implies wrongness of the other party. The following are some of the basic human needs we all share:

Autonomy

- to choose one's dreams, goals, and values
- to choose one's plan for fulfilling one's dreams, goals, and values

Celebration

- to celebrate the creation of life and dreams fulfilled
- to celebrate losses: loved ones, dreams, etc. (mourning)

Integrity

- authenticity
- creativity
- meaning
- self-worth

Interdependence

- acceptance
- appreciation
- closeness

Interdependence continued

- community
- consideration
- contribution to the enrichment of life (to exercise one's power by giving that which contributes to life)
- emotional safety
- empathy
- honesty (the empowering honesty that enables us to learn from our limitations)
- love
- reassurance
- respect
- support
- trust
- understanding
- warmth

Physical Nurturance

- air
- food
- movement, exercise

Physical Nurturance continued

- protection from life-threatening forms of life: viruses, bacteria, insects, predatory animals, etc.
- rest
- sexual expression
- shelter
- touch
- water

Play

- fun
- laughter

Spiritual Communion

- beauty
- harmony
- inspiration
- order
- peace

Unfortunately, I've found that very few people are literate in expressing needs. Instead they have been trained to criticize, insult, and otherwise communicate in ways that create distance among people. As a result, even in conflicts for which resolutions exist, resolutions are not found. And instead of both parties expressing their own needs and understanding the needs of the other party, both sides play the game of who's right. That game is more likely to end in various forms of verbal, psychological, or physical violence than in peaceful resolution of differences.

Since needs are such a vital component of this approach to conflict resolution, I'd like to clarify what I'm referring to when I talk about needs. *Needs*, as I use the term, can be thought of as resources life requires to sustain itself. For example, our physical well-being depends on our needs for air, water, rest, and food being fulfilled. Our psychological and spiritual well-being is enhanced when our needs for understanding, support, honesty, and meaning are fulfilled.

As I'm defining needs, all human beings have the same needs. Regardless of our gender, educational level, religious beliefs. or nationality, we have the same needs. What differs from person to person is the strategy for fulfilling needs. I've found that it facilitates conflict resolution to keep our needs separate from the strategies that might fulfill our needs.

One guideline for separating needs from strategies is to keep in mind that needs contain no reference to specific people taking specific action. In contrast, effective strategies—or what are more commonly referred to as wants, requests, desires, and "solutions"—*do* refer to specific people taking specific actions. An exchange between a husband and wife who had just about given up on their marriage will clarify this important difference between needs and strategies.

I asked the husband what needs of his were not being fulfilled in the marriage. He responded, "I need to get out of this relationship." Since he was talking about a specific person (himself) taking specific action (leaving the marriage) he was not expressing a need as I define needs. Instead he was telling me a strategy that he was thinking of taking. I pointed this out to him and suggested that we delay talking about strategies until we had really clarified both his needs and the needs of his wife. When they were able to clarify their needs, both saw that there were other strategies besides ending the relationship that could meet their needs. And I'm pleased to say that in the two years since that time, they've developed a relationship within the marriage that is very satisfactory to both.

Many people find it difficult to express needs. This lack of "need literacy" creates problems when people want to resolve conflicts. As an example, I would like to tell you about a husband and wife whose attempts to resolve conflicts had led them to visit physical violence upon one another.

I had been working in the husband's workplace offering some training, and at the end of the training, the husband asked me if he could talk to me privately. He tearfully expressed the situation between his wife and himself, and asked if I would meet with them to support them in resolving some of their conflicts. The wife agreed, and so I went there that evening.

I began by saying: "I'm aware that you're both in a lot of pain. I would suggest that we begin with each of you expressing whatever needs of yours are not being fulfilled in the relationship. Once you've understood one another's needs, I'm confident we can explore some strategies to meet those needs."

What I was asking them both required a literacy of expressing needs and an ability to understand one another's needs.

Unfortunately, they weren't able to do as I suggested. They didn't have the literacy. Instead of expressing his needs, the husband said, "The problem with you is that you're totally insensitive to my needs." Immediately his wife responded by saying, "That's typical of you to say unfair things like that."

Another time I was working within a company that had a very disturbing conflict for more than fifteen months that was creating morale as well as productivity problems. In this conflict there were two different factions within the same department. The conflict involved which piece of software to use. There were strong emotions involved. One faction had worked very hard to develop the software that was presently in use, and they wanted to continue its use. The other faction had strong emotions tied up in a new piece of software.

When I met with this group, I started in the same way as with the husband and wife. I asked both sides to tell me what their needs were that would be better fulfilled with the software they advocated. As in the situation with the husband and wife, I didn't receive a clear expression of needs. Instead, each side responded with an intellectual analysis that the other side received as criticism.

A member from one faction said, "I think that if we continue to be overly conservative, we could be out of work in the future, because to be progressive requires that we take some risks, and dare to show that we are beyond old fashioned ways of doing things." A member of the other faction responded, "But I think that impulsively grabbing for every new thing that comes along is not in our best interest." They told me that they had been repeating these same analyses of one another for months, and getting nowhere. In fact, they were creating a lot of tension among themselves.

Like the husband and wife, they didn't know how to directly express their needs. Instead they were making analyses and were being heard by the other side as critical. This is how wars are created. When we're not able to say clearly what we need and only know how to make analyses of others that sound like criticism, wars are never far away, whether they are verbal, psychological, or physical wars.

Sensing the Needs of Others
(No Matter How They Express Themselves)

The approach to conflict resolution that I am describing requires not only that we learn to express our needs, but also that we assist others in clarifying their needs. We can train ourselves to hear needs being expressed through the messages of others, regardless of how others are expressing themselves.

I've taught myself to do this because I believe that every message, whatever its form or content, is an expression of a need. If we accept this assumption, we can train ourselves to sense what needs might be at the root of any particular message. Thus, if I ask someone a question about what they have just said, and they respond, "That's a stupid question," I choose to sense what the other person might need as expressed through that particular judgment of me. For example, I might guess that their need for understanding was not being fulfilled when I asked that particular question.

Or, if I request that someone talk with me about some stress in our relationship and they say, "I don't want to talk about it," I might sense that their need is for protection from what they imagine might happen if we communicate.

This ability to sense what people need is crucial in mediating conflicts. We can help by sensing what both sides need, put it into words, and then we help each side hear the other side's needs. This creates a quality of connection that moves the conflict to successful resolution.

Let me give you an example of what I mean. I often work with groups of married couples. In these groups, I identify the couple with the most long-standing conflict, and I make a rather startling prediction to the group. I predict that we will be able to resolve this long-standing conflict within twenty minutes from the point at which both sides can tell me what the other side needs.

Once when I was doing this with a group, we identified a couple married for thirty-nine years. They had a conflict about money. Six months into the marriage the wife had twice overdrawn the checkbook, and the husband had taken control of the checkbook and wouldn't let her write checks from that point on. They had been arguing about this for thirty-nine years.

When the wife heard my prediction she said: "Marshall, I can tell you this, that's not going to happen. I mean, we have a good marriage, we communicate quite well, but in this conflict, we just have different needs about money. I don't see how it can possibly be resolved in twenty minutes."

I corrected her by saying that I hadn't predicted we'd resolve it in twenty minutes. "I predicted resolution within twenty minutes after both of you tell me what the other person needs." She said, "But Marshall, we communicate very well, and when you have been talking about something for thirty-nine years, you certainly understand what the other side needs."

I responded, "Well, I've been wrong before. I certainly could be wrong in this situation, but let's explore. Tell me then, if you know what his needs are, what are they?"

She said, "It's very obvious, Marshall. He doesn't want me to spend any money."

The husband immediately reacted by saying, "That's ridiculous."

It was clear that she and I had a different definition of needs. When she said he didn't want her to spend any money, she was identifying what I call a strategy. Even if she was right, she would have been accurate about his desired *strategy,* not about his *need.* As I define needs, a need contains no reference to specific actions such as spending money or not spending money.

I told her that all human beings have the same needs, and I was certain that if she could get clear what her husband's needs were, and if he were clear about her needs, we could resolve this. I said: "Can you try again? What do you think his need is?"

And she said: "Well, let me explain, Marshall. You see, he's just like his own father." And then she told me how his father was reluctant to spend money. I stopped her and said: "Hold on now. You're giving me an analysis of why he is the way he is. What I am asking is to simply tell me what need of his is involved in this situation. You're giving me an intellectual analysis of what has gone on in his life."

It was very clear that she didn't know how to identify his need. Even after thirty-nine years of talking, she still didn't have an idea what his needs were. She had diagnoses of him, she had an intellectual awareness of what his reasons might be for not wanting her to have the checkbook, but she didn't really understand his needs in this situation.

So I asked the husband: "Well, since your wife is not in touch with what your needs are, why don't you tell her? What are your needs that are being met by keeping the checkbook yourself?"

He said: "Marshall, she's a wonderful wife, a wonderful mother. But when it comes to money, she's totally irresponsible."

Now again, notice the difference between the question I asked him, "What are your needs in this situation," and his response. Instead of telling me what his needs were, he gave me a diagnosis that she was irresponsible. It's that kind of language that I believe gets in the way of resolving conflicts peacefully. At the point where either party hears themselves criticized, diagnosed, or intellectually interpreted, I predict their energy will turn toward self-defense and counter-accusations rather than toward resolutions that meet everyone's needs.

I pointed out to him that he was not really in touch with what his needs were and I showed that he was giving me a diagnosis of his wife instead. Then I again asked him, "What are your needs in this situation?" He couldn't identify them.

So even after thirty-nine years of discussion, neither person was really aware of the other person's needs. Here was a situation where my ability to sense needs could help them out of conflict. I used Nonviolent Communication skills to guess the *needs* that the husband and wife were expressing as judgments.

I reminded him that he had said his wife was totally irresponsible about money (a judgment), and then I asked, "Are you feeling scared in this situation because you have a need to protect the family economically?" When I said this, he looked at me and said, "That's exactly what I'm saying." Of course he didn't say exactly that! But when we sense what a person needs, I believe that we're getting closer to the truth, closer to what people are trying to say. I believe that all analysis that implies wrongness is basically a tragic expression of unmet needs. If we can hear what a person needs, it's a great gift to them because it helps them to get connected to life.

Now, I happened to guess right in this situation, but it didn't require that I guess right. If I had been off, at least I was focusing his attention on needs, and that helps people get more in touch with their needs. It takes them out of the analysis and gets them more connected to life.

Checking to See That Needs Are Accurately Received

Once he had expressed his need, the next step was to be sure that the other person heard it. This is a crucial skill in conflict resolution. We can't assume that, just because a message is expressed, the other person receives it accurately. Whenever I am mediating a conflict, if I am not sure that the person hearing the message has accurately received it, I ask them to repeat it back.

I asked his wife, "Could you tell me back what you heard your husband's needs are in this situation?"

And she said, "Well, just because I overdrew the bank account a couple of times when we got married, that doesn't mean I'm going to continue doing it."

Her response was not atypical in my experience. When people have pain built up over many years, even when the other person says clearly what they need, it doesn't mean the first person can hear it. Often they're so filled with their own pain that it gets in the way of their hearing another.

I asked her if she could possibly repeat back what the husband said, but it was clear that she really hadn't heard it, that she was in too much pain. I said to her, "I would like to tell you what I heard your husband say, and I would like you to repeat it back," and I repeated it for her. I said: "I heard that your husband says he has a need to protect the family. He's scared because he really wants to be sure that the family is protected."

Providing Empathy to Heal the Pain (That Prevents People From Hearing Each Other)

Because she still couldn't hear it, I used another skill that is often necessary in conflict resolution. I shifted. Instead of trying to get her to repeat what he'd said I tried to understand the pain that she felt.

I said, "I sense that you're feeling really hurt, and you need to be trusted that you can learn from past experience." You could tell from her eyes that she really needed that understanding, and she said, "Yes, exactly."

Having received this understanding, I hoped that she would now be able to hear her husband, so once again I repeated what I understood his needs to be. He needed to protect the family. I asked her to repeat back what she heard. She replied, "So he thinks I'm spending too much money."

Well, as you see, she wasn't trained to hear needs any more than she was trained to express them. Instead of hearing his needs, all she heard was a diagnosis of herself. I suggested that she try to just hear the needs, without hearing any criticism of herself in it. After I repeated it two more times, she was finally able to hear her husband's needs.

Then I reversed the process and asked the wife to express her needs. Again, she wasn't able to do it directly; she expressed her need in the form of a judgment and said: "He doesn't trust me. He thinks I'm stupid and that I'm not going to be able to learn. I think that's unfair. I mean, just because I did it a couple of times doesn't mean I'll continue to do it."

Once again I loaned her the skill of my being able to sense her needs behind all of that. I said to her: "It sounds like you really have a need to be trusted. You really want acknowledgment that you can learn from the situation."

Then I asked the husband to tell me what his wife's needs were. And, just as she had judgments that kept her from hearing him at first, he couldn't hear her. He wanted to defend his need to protect the family and began to explain that she was a good wife, a good mother, but that she was just totally irresponsible when it came to money. I had to help him hear through his judgment, to just hear what her needs were, so I said, "Would you please just tell me what her needs are?" He had to have it repeated three times, but finally he heard her need was to be trusted.

Then, as I had predicted, at the point when they both had heard each other's needs, it didn't take twenty minutes to find a way of getting everybody's needs met. It took much less time than that!

The more I have been involved in conflicts over the years, the more I've seen that what leads families to argue—what lead nations to war—the more I believe that most schoolchildren could resolve these conflicts. If people just asked: "Here are the needs of both sides, here are the resources. What can be done to meet these needs?" the conflict would be easy to resolve. But tragically, we're not taught to think in terms of the human needs involved, and our thinking does not go to that level. Instead it goes to dehumanizing one another with labels and judgments, and then even the simplest of conflicts become very difficult to solve.

Resolving Disputes Between Groups of People

To show how these same principles can apply when there are more than two people involved, let's examine a conflict I was asked to mediate between two tribes in Nigeria. These tribes had had enormous violence going on between them for the previous year. In fact, one fourth of their population was killed, one hundred out of four hundred people dead, in one year.

Seeing this violence, a colleague of mine who lives in Nigeria worked hard to get the chiefs on both sides to agree to meet with me to see if we could resolve the conflict. After much effort, he finally got them to agree.

As we were walking into the session, my colleague whispered to me: "Be prepared for a little bit of tension, Marshall. Three of the people in the room know that the person who killed their child is in that room."

Well, it was very tense at first. There had been so much violence between these two groups, and it was the first time they had really sat down together.

I started with the question I frequently start conflict resolution sessions with, to focus on people's needs. I said to both sides: "I'd like whoever would like to speak first to say what your needs are in this situation. After everyone understands the needs of everyone else, then we'll move to finding some ways of meeting the needs."

Unfortunately, like the husband and wife, they didn't have a literacy of needs—they only knew how to tell me what was wrong with the other side. Instead of responding to my question, the chief from one side looked across the table and said, "You people are murderers," and the other side responded: "You've been trying to dominate us. We're not going to tolerate it anymore!" We had more tension after two sentences than we had when it began.

Obviously, just getting people together to communicate doesn't help, unless they know how to communicate in a way that connects them as human beings. My job was the same as it was with the married couple: loan them the ability to sense needs behind whatever is being expressed.

I turned to the chief who had said, "You people are murderers," and guessed, "Chief, do you have a need for safety, and to be sure that whatever conflicts are going on will be resolved by some means other than violence?" The chief immediately said to me, "Of course, of course that's what I'm saying!" Well, of course he didn't say that. He said that the other person was a murderer, and made a judgment rather than express his needs. However, we had his needs out on the table so I turned to a chief from the other side and said, "Chief, would you please reflect back what he said his needs were?"

The chief responded to this man by asking in a very hostile way, "Then why did you kill my son?"

That started an uproar between the two groups. After things calmed down, I said: "Chief, we'll deal with your reaction to his needs later, but at the moment I suggest that you just hear his needs. Could you tell me back what he said his needs were?" He couldn't do it. He was so emotionally involved in this situation and in his judgments of the other person that he didn't hear what the other person's needs were. I repeated the needs as I heard them and said: "Chief, I heard the other chief saying that he has a need for safety. He has a need to feel secure, that no matter what conflicts are present, they'll be resolved in some way other than by violence. Could you just reflect back what that need is, so that I'm sure everybody's communicating?" He couldn't do it. I had to repeat it two or three times before he could hear the other person's needs.

I reversed the process and said to the second chief: "I thank you for hearing that he has this need for security. Now I'd like to hear what your needs are in this." He said: "They have been trying to dominate us. They are a dominating group of people. They think they're better than everybody." Once again, this started a fight with the other side. I had to interrupt and say, "Excuse me, excuse me." After the group settled, I went back to trying to sense the needs behind his statement that the other side was dominating.

I asked: "Chief, is your need behind that statement a need for equality? You really need to feel that you're being treated equally in this community?" And he said, "Yes, of course!"

Now again, the job was to get the chief on the other side to hear, which wasn't easy. It took three or four repetitions before I could get the chief on the other side just to see the need that this human being was expressing. Finally the chief was able to hear the other chief saying he had a need for equality.

After I spent this much time getting both sides to express their needs and to hear each other's needs (this took close to two hours), another chief who hadn't spoken jumped to his feet, looked at me and said something very intensely. I didn't speak his language, so I was very curious what he was trying to express to me with such intensity, and eagerly awaited the translation. I was very touched when the translator said: "The chief says we cannot learn this way of communicating in one day. And he says, if we know how to communicate this way, we don't have to kill each other."

I said to the translator: "Tell the chief I am very grateful that he sees what can happen when we hear each other's needs. Tell him that today my objective was to help resolve the conflict peacefully to everyone's satisfaction, and I was hoping that people could see the value in this way of communicating. Tell him that if people on both sides would like, we will be glad to train people within each tribe to communicate this way, so that future conflicts could be resolved this way rather than through violence."

That chief wanted to be one of the members to be trained, and in fact before I left that day, we had members from both tribes eager to learn this process that would allow everyone's to hear needs behind whatever message was being expressed. I am happy to report that the war between the tribes ended that day.

Offering Strategies in Positive Action Language

After we have helped parties in a conflict express their needs and connect with the needs of others, then I suggest we move on to look for strategies that meet everyone's needs. In my experience, if we move too quickly to strategies, we may find some compromises, but we won't have the same quality of resolution. If we thoroughly understand needs before moving to proposed solutions, we increase the likelihood that both parties will stay with the agreement.

Of course, it's not enough just to help each side see what the other side needs. We must end with action, action that meets everyone's needs. This requires that we be able to express proposed strategies clearly in present, positive action language.

By "present" language I mean a clear statement of what is wanted from the other side *at this moment*, such as "I'd like you to tell me if you would be willing to . . . ," and then say the action that you would like the other person to take. Bringing it into the present by saying, "Would you be willing to . . . " makes it easier to foster a respectful discussion. If the other side says they are not willing, we can find out why not. I've found that the conflicts move more toward resolution if we can learn to say the request in present language.

If we say to someone, "I'd like you to go to the show with me Saturday night," it's pretty clear what I want on Saturday night, but that doesn't necessarily make clear what I want from the person at that moment. I might want at the moment for the person to tell me if they would be willing to go. I may want them to tell me how they feel about going with me. I might want them to tell me whether they have any reservations about going, and so forth.

The more we can be clear what response we're wanting *right now*, the more quickly conflict moves toward resolution.

I also suggest that requests be expressed in *positive action language* by stating clearly what we want done to meet our needs, rather than what we don't want. In conflict situations, telling people what we don't want creates both confusion and resistance. This applies even when we're talking to ourselves. If we just tell ourselves what we don't want to do, we're not likely to make much change in the situation.

I can think of a time several years ago when I was debating an issue on public television. The program was taped earlier in the day so it could be shown in the evening, and I was able to go home and watch it. While I was watching this program, I became very upset with myself because I was doing three things I don't like doing when I'm debating. So I remember saying to myself, "If I'm ever debating an issue like this again, I don't want to do A, I don't want to do B, I don't want to do C."

I had a chance to redeem myself because the following week I was asked to continue the same debate. As I was going to the television station I repeated to myself, "Now remember, don't do A, don't do B, and don't do C." I got on the program, the other debater came at me the same way he had been communicating the previous week, and what did I do? For ten seconds I was beautiful. And what did I do after ten seconds? A, B, and C. In fact, as I recall, I quickly made up for the lost ten seconds!

The problem was that I told myself what *not* to do. I hadn't gotten clear about exactly what I wanted to do differently. So, in conflict resolution, it helps both parties to say clearly what they do want—rather than what they don't want—in order to meet everyone's needs.

A woman made this point very clear to me one time. She had a conflict with her husband about how much time he was spending at home, and said to him, "I don't want you spending so much time at work." Afterwards she got furious with him when he signed up for a bowling league! Here again, she said what she didn't want, not what she did want. If she had expressed what she did want, it might have sounded like this, "I'd like you to tell me if you'd be willing to spend at least one evening a week with the children and me."

Action language means saying clearly what we do want when we make a request, using clear action verbs. It also means avoiding language that obscures our needs or sounds like an attack.

For example, one couple had had a conflict for twelve years. The woman had a need for understanding that wasn't being met in the relationship. When I got her partner to reflect her need, I said, "Okay, now let's get down to strategies." I asked, "What do you want, from him for example, to meet your need for understanding?" She looked at her husband and replied, "I'd like you to listen to me when I talk to you." He said, "I do listen." and she said, "No you don't." And he said, "Yes I do." They told me they'd had this same conversation for twelve years. This is what happens when we use words like "listen" to express our strategies. It's too vague. It's not an action verb.

With my help, this woman realized what she really wanted from her partner when she said, "I want you to listen." She wanted him to reflect back what she was saying, so that she could be sure she had made herself clear. When she made that positive action request of him, he was quite willing to do it. She was delighted because this strategy really met her need. Finally she was getting a need met that she had been very eager to have met for twelve years. All she was lacking was clear language for telling him what she wanted.

A similar husband-and-wife conflict involved the wife's need that her husband respect her choices. Once her husband understood, I said: "Now that your husband understands your need to have your choices respected, what are you requesting of him? What are your strategies for getting that need met?"

She said, "Well, I want you to give me the freedom to grow and be myself," and he replied, "I do." She responded, "No you don't" and he said, "I do." Then I said, "Hold it, hold on!"

Once again we see non-action language exacerbating a conflict. People can easily hear, "Give me the freedom to grow" as implying that they are a slave-master or domineering. This request doesn't make clear what IS wanted. So I pointed this out to her. I said, "I'd like you to tell him exactly what you want him to do to better meet your need for having your choices respected."

She replied, "I want you to allow me . . . " and I stopped her and said: "I'm afraid that *allow* is vague also. Can you use a more concrete action verb than allow?"

She replied, "Well, how about if I want him to let me?" "No," I said: "That's still pretty vague. What do you really mean when you say you want a person to let you?"

After thinking it over for a few seconds, she came to an important awareness. She said: "Uh oh, Marshall, I see what's going on. I'm clear what I want from him when I say 'I want you to let me be' and 'I want you to give me the freedom to grow.' If I say this in clear language I'd have to say it this way, and it's pretty embarrassing. Besides, I can see that he couldn't do it. I want him to tell me it's okay no matter what I do."

When she got clear about what she was actually requesting, she saw that it didn't leave him much freedom to be himself and to have *his* choices respected.

Respect is a key element of successful conflict resolution.

Resolving Conflicts With Authorities

I was working with a group of minority students in a southern city many years ago. They had the impression that the principal of their school was very racist in many of his behaviors, and wanted my help in developing skills to resolve their conflicts with him.

When we worked in our training session, they defined their needs clearly. When we talked about expressing their request, they said: "Marshall, we're not optimistic about making requests of him. We did make requests of him in the past, and it wasn't very pleasant. In the past, he has said, 'Get out of here or I'm going to call the police.'" I asked, "What request did you make of him?"

One of the students replied, "We said we didn't want him telling us how we could wear our hair." They were referring to the fact that the principal barred them from the football team unless they cut their hair short. I pointed out to them: "Telling him what you don't want (you don't want him telling you how to wear your hair) is really not what I'm suggesting. I'm suggesting you learn how to tell him what you do want."

Another student said, "Well, we told him we wanted fairness." I responded: "Well, that's a need. We have a need for fairness. Once we know our needs, the next step is to be clear with people about what we really want them to do. What can they do to meet our needs? We have to learn how to say that more clearly."

We worked very hard and came up with thirty-eight present requests in positive action language, and we practiced how to present their requests in a respectful, nondemanding way. Doing that means that after you make your request, no matter how the other person responds, whether the person says yes or no, you give an equal amount of respect and understanding. If they say "no," try to understand *what need they are meeting* that keeps them from saying "yes."

Respecting Is Not the Same as Conceding

Understanding the other person's needs does not mean you have to give up your own needs. It does mean demonstrating to the other person that you are interested in *both* your needs *and* theirs. When they trust that, there's much more likelihood of everyone's needs getting met, which is what happened in this situation.

The students went in, told the principal their needs, and expressed their thirty-eight requests in clear action language. They listened to what needs the principal had, and in the end the principal agreed to all thirty-eight of their requests.

About two weeks after that happened, I got a call from a representative of the school district asking if I would teach their school administrator what I had taught those students.

It's very important, in expressing our requests, to be respectful of the other person's reaction regardless of whether they agree to the request. One of the most important messages another person can give us is "no" or "I don't want to." If we listen well to this message, it helps us understand the other person's needs. If we are listening to other peoples' needs, we will see that every time a person says "no," they're really saying they have a need that is not addressed by our strategy, which keeps them from saying "yes." If we can teach ourselves to hear the need behind that "no," we will find an openness toward getting everyone's needs met.

Of course, if we hear the "no" as a rejection, or if we start to blame the other person for saying "no," then it's not likely that we're going to find a way of getting everyone's needs met. It's key that, throughout the process, we keep everyone's attention focused on *meeting everyone's needs.*

I'm very optimistic about what happens in any conflict if we create this quality of connection. If all sides in a conflict get clear about what they need and hear the other side's needs, if people express their strategies in clear action language, then even if the other person says "no," the focus returns to meeting *needs.* If we all do this, we will easily find strategies that get everyone's needs met.

When You Can't Get the Two Sides Together

So I'm very optimistic what can happen when you can get people together and talking at this level, but of course that requires getting them together. In recent years, I have been looking for strategies for resolving conflicts when we can't get both sides together.

One strategy that I'm very pleased with involves the use of a tape recorder. I work with each party separately, and play the role of the other person. Here's what this looks like.

A woman came to me very much in pain because of the conflict between her and her husband, especially because of how he was handling his anger and beating her at times. She wanted him to come to the meeting with her and talk about this conflict that they had, but he refused. When she came into my office, I said, "Let me play the role of your husband." In that role I listened to what she was saying and respectfully heard the feelings that she was expressing, how it felt to her to be hit and to not be understood as she would like.

I listened in a way that helped her get her needs more clearly expressed and showed a respectful understanding of her needs. Then in the role of the husband, I expressed what I guessed the husband's needs were, and asked her to hear me. We audio-taped this role-play between the husband and the wife, with me playing the role of the husband, and with my help we had clearly communicated the needs. Then I asked her to take this tape to her husband and get his reaction to it.

When she took the tape to her husband and he heard how I played his role, he felt a good deal of relief. Apparently, I had guessed accurately what his needs were. As a result of the understanding that he felt by how I had empathically played his role, he did come in and we continued to work together until they found other ways of meeting their needs besides violence.

Conclusion

I've been sharing some of my concepts of conflict resolution, showing how much I believe a literacy of needs helps, how important it is to both express needs, and to hear the other side's needs, and then to look for strategies and to express them using clear action language.

I hope what I've shared supports you to resolve any personal conflicts more harmoniously, and that it also supports your efforts to mediate the conflicts of others. I hope it strengthens your awareness of the precious flow of communication that allows conflicts to be resolved so that everyone's needs are fulfilled. I also hope that it increases your awareness of the possibility of communication that precludes the necessity of coercion, a flow of communication that increases our awareness of our interdependence.

The Four-Part Nonviolent Communication Process

Clearly expressing
how **I am**
without blaming
or criticizing

Empathically receiving
how **you are**
without hearing
blame or criticism

OBSERVATIONS

1. What I observe *(see, hear, remember, imagine, free from my evaluations)* that does or does not contribute to my well-being:

   "When I (see, hear) . . . "

1. What you observe *(see, hear, remember, imagine, free from your evaluations)* that does or does not contribute to your well-being:

   "When you see/hear . . . "

   (Sometimes unspoken when offering empathy)

FEELINGS

2. How I feel *(emotion or sensation rather than thought)* in relation to what I observe:

   "I feel . . . "

2. How you feel *(emotion or sensation rather than thought)* in relation to what you observe:

   "You feel . . ."

NEEDS

3. What I need or value *(rather than a preference, or a specific action)* that causes my feelings:

   " . . . because I need/value . . . "

3. What you need or value *(rather than a preference, or a specific action)* that causes your feelings:

   " . . . because you need/value . . ."

Clearly requesting that
which would enrich **my**
life without demanding

Empathically receiving that
which would enrich **your** life
without hearing any demand

REQUESTS

4. The concrete actions I would like taken:

   "Would you be willing to . . . ?"

4. The concrete actions you would like taken:

   "Would you like . . . ?"

   (Sometimes unspoken when offering empathy)

© Marshall B. Rosenberg. For more information about Marshall B. Rosenberg or the Center for Nonviolent Communication, please visit www.CNVC.org.

Some Basic Feelings We All Have

Feelings when needs are fulfilled

- Amazed
- Comfortable
- Confident
- Eager
- Energetic
- Fulfilled
- Glad
- Hopeful
- Inspired
- Intrigued
- Joyous
- Moved
- Optimistic
- Proud
- Relieved
- Stimulated
- Surprised
- Thankful
- Touched
- Trustful

Feelings when needs are not fulfilled

- Angry
- Annoyed
- Concerned
- Confused
- Disappointed
- Discouraged
- Distressed
- Embarrassed
- Frustrated
- Helpless
- Hopeless
- Impatient
- Irritated
- Lonely
- Nervous
- Overwhelmed
- Puzzled
- Reluctant
- Sad
- Uncomfortable

Some Basic Needs We All Have

Autonomy
- Choosing dreams/goals/values
- Choosing plans for fulfilling one's dreams, goals, values

Celebration
- Celebrating the creation of life and dreams fulfilled
- Celebrating losses: loved ones, dreams, etc. (mourning)

Integrity
- Authenticity • Creativity
- Meaning • Self-worth

Interdependence
- Acceptance • Appreciation
- Closeness • Community
- Consideration
- Contribution to the enrichment of life
- Emotional Safety • Empathy

Physical Nurturance
- Air • Food
- Movement, exercise
- Protection from life-threatening forms of life: viruses, bacteria, insects, predatory animals
- Rest • Sexual Expression
- Shelter • Touch • Water

Play
- Fun • Laughter

Spiritual Communion
- Beauty • Harmony
- Inspiration • Order • Peace

- Honesty (the empowering honesty that enables us to learn from our limitations)
- Love • Reassurance
- Respect • Support
- Trust • Understanding

About PuddleDancer Press

PuddleDancer Press (PDP) is the premier publisher of Nonviolent Communication™ related works. Its mission is to provide high-quality materials to help people create a world in which all needs are met compassionately. Publishing revenues are used to develop new books, and implement promotion campaigns for NVC and Marshall Rosenberg. By working in partnership with the Center for Nonviolent Communication and NVC trainers, teams, and local supporters, PDP has created a comprehensive promotion effort that has helped bring NVC to thousands of new people each year.

Since 2003 PDP has donated more than 60,000 NVC books to organizations, decision-makers, and individuals in need around the world. This program is supported in part by donations made to CNVC and by partnerships with like-minded organizations around the world.

Visit the PDP website at www.NonviolentCommunication.com to find the following resources:

- **Shop NVC**—Continue your learning. Purchase our NVC titles online safely, affordably, and conveniently. Find everyday discounts on individual titles, multiple-copies, and book packages. Learn more about our authors and read endorsements of NVC from world-renowned communication experts and peacemakers. www.NonviolentCommunication.com/store/

- **NVC Quick Connect e-Newsletter**—Sign up today to receive our monthly e-Newsletter, filled with expert articles, upcoming training opportunities with our authors, and exclusive specials on NVC learning materials. Archived e-Newsletters are also available

- **About NVC**—Learn more about these life-changing communication and conflict resolution skills including an overview of the NVC process, key facts about NVC, and more.

- **About Marshall Rosenberg**—Access press materials, biography, and more about this world-renowned peacemaker, educator, bestselling author, and founder of the Center for Nonviolent Communication.

- **Free Resources for Learning NVC**—Find free weekly tips series, NVC article archive, and other great resources to make learning these vital communication skills just a little easier.

 *PuddleDancer* PRESS

For more information, please contact PuddleDancer Press at:

2240 Encinitas Blvd., Ste. D-911 • Encinitas, CA 92024
Phone: 760-652-5754 • Fax: 760-274-6400
Email: email@puddledancer.com • www.NonviolentCommunication.com

The Center for Nonviolent Communication (CNVC) is an international nonprofit peacemaking organization whose vision is a world where everyone's needs are met peacefully. CNVC is devoted to supporting the spread of Nonviolent Communication (NVC) around the world.

Founded in 1984 by Dr. Marshall B. Rosenberg, CNVC has been contributing to a vast social transformation in thinking, speaking and acting—showing people how to connect in ways that inspire compassionate results. NVC is now being taught around the globe in communities, schools, prisons, mediation centers, churches, businesses, professional conferences, and more. More than 200 certified trainers and hundreds more teach NVC to approximately 250,000 people each year in 35 countries.

CNVC believes that NVC training is a crucial step to continue building a compassionate, peaceful society. Your tax-deductible donation will help CNVC continue to provide training in some of the most impoverished, violent corners of the world. It will also support the development and continuation of organized projects aimed at bringing NVC training to high-need geographic regions and populations.

To make a tax-deductible donation or to learn more about the valuable resources described below, visit the CNVC website at www.CNVC.org:

- **Training and Certification**—Find local, national, and international training opportunities, access trainer certification information, connect to local NVC communities, trainers, and more.

- **CNVC Bookstore**—Find mail or phone order information for a complete selection of NVC books, booklets, audio, and video materials at the CNVC website.

- **CNVC Projects**—Seven regional and theme-based projects provide focus and leadership for teaching NVC in a particular application or geographic region.

- **E-Groups and List Servs**—Join one of several moderated, topic-based NVC e-groups and list servs developed to support individual learning and the continued growth of NVC worldwide.

For more information, please contact CNVC at:

5600 San Francisco Rd., NE, Suite A, Albuquerque, NM 87109
Ph: 505-244-4041 • Fax: 505-247-0414
Email: cnvc@CNVC.org • Website: www.CNVC.org

Peaceful Living

*Daily Meditations for Living With Love,
Healing, and Compassion*

by Mary Mackenzie

$19.95 — Trade Paper 5x7.5, 448pp
ISBN: 978-1-892005-19-9

In this gathering of wisdom, Mary Mackenzie empowers you with an intimate life map that will literally change the course of your life for the better. Each of the 366 meditations includes an inspirational quote and concrete, practical tips for integrating the daily message into your life. The learned behaviors of cynicism, resentment, and getting even are replaced with the skills of Nonviolent Communication, including recognizing one's needs and values and making choices in alignment with them.

Peaceful Living goes beyond daily affirmations, providing the skills and consciousness you need to transform relationships, heal pain, and discover the life-enriching meaning behind even the most trying situations. Begin each day centered and connected to yourself and your values. Direct the course of your life toward your deepest hopes and needs. Ground yourself in the power of compassionate, conscious living.

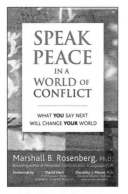

Speak Peace in a World of Conflict

What You Say Next Will Change Your World

by Marshall B. Rosenberg, Ph.D.

$15.95 — Trade Paper 5-3/8x8-3/8, 208pp
ISBN: 978-1-892005-17-5

International peacemaker, mediator, and healer, Marshall Rosenberg shows you how the language you use is the key to enriching life. *Speak Peace* is filled with inspiring stories, lessons, and ideas drawn from more than forty years of mediating conflicts and healing relationships in some of the most war-torn, impoverished, and violent corners of the world. Find insight, practical skills, and powerful tools that will profoundly change your relationships and the course of your life for the better.

Discover how you can create an internal consciousness of peace as the first step toward effective personal, professional, and social change. Find complete chapters on the mechanics of Speaking Peace, conflict resolution, transforming business culture, transforming enemy images, addressing terrorism, transforming authoritarian structures, expressing and receiving gratitude, and social change.

Nonviolent Communication has flourished for four decades across thirty-five countries selling more than 1,000,000 books in more than twenty-five languages for one simple reason: it works.

Available from PuddleDancer Press, the Center for Nonviolent Communication, all major bookstores, and Amazon.com. Distributed by Independent Publisher's Group: 800-888-4741.

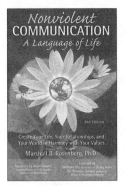

Nonviolent Communication:
A Language of Life, Second Edition
*Create Your Life, Your Relationships, and Your World
in Harmony With Your Values*
Marshall B. Rosenberg, Ph.D.
$19.95 — Trade Paper 6x9, 240pp
ISBN: 978-1-892005-03-8

In this internationally acclaimed text, Marshall Rosenberg offers insightful stories, anecdotes, practical exercises, and role-plays that will literally change your approach to communication for the better. Nonviolent Communication partners practical skills with a powerful consciousness to help us get what we want peacefully.

Nonviolent Communication has flourished for four decades across thirty-five countries selling more than 1,000,000 books in more than twenty-five languages for one simple reason: it works.

"Nonviolent Communication is a simple yet powerful methodology for communicating in a way that meets both parties' needs. This is one of the most useful books you will ever read."
　　—William Ury, coauthor of *Getting to Yes* and author of *The Third Side*

"I believe the principles and techniques in this book can literally change the world."
　　—Jack Canfield, author, *Chicken Soup for the Soul*

Nonviolent Communication
Companion Workbook
*A Practical Guide for Individual,
Group, or Classroom Study*

by Lucy Leu

$21.95 — Trade Paper 7x10, 224pp
ISBN: 978-1-892005-04-5

Learning Nonviolent Communication has often been equated with learning a whole new language. The *NVC Companion Workbook* helps you put these powerful, effective skills into practice with chapter-by-chapter study of Marshall Rosenberg's cornerstone text, *NVC: A Language of Life*. Create a safe, supportive group learning or practice environment that nurtures the needs of each participant. Find a wealth of activities, exercises, and facilitator suggestions to refine and practice this powerful communication process.

Nonviolent Communication has flourished for four decades across thirty-five countries selling more than 1,000,000 books in more than twenty-five languages for one simple reason: it works.

Available from PuddleDancer Press, the Center for Nonviolent Communication, all major bookstores, and Amazon.com. Distributed by Independent Publisher's Group: 800-888-4741.

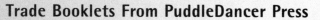

Being Me, Loving You: *A Practical Guide to Extraordinary Relationships* **by Marshall B. Rosenberg, Ph.D.** • Watch your relationships strengthen as you learn to think of love as something you "do," something you give freely from the heart. 80pp • **$8.95**

Getting Past the Pain Between Us: *Healing and Reconciliation Without Compromise* **by Marshall B. Rosenberg, Ph.D.** • Learn simple steps to create the heartfelt presence necessary for lasting healing to occur—great for mediators, counselors, families, and couples. 48pp • **$8.95**

Graduating From Guilt: *Six Steps to Overcome Guilt and Reclaim Your Life* **by Holly Michelle Eckert** • The burden of guilt leaves us stuck, stressed, and feeling like we can never measure up. Through a proven six-step process, this book helps liberate you from the toxic guilt, blame, and shame you carry. 96pp • **$9.95**

Humanizing Health Care: *Creating Cultures of Compassion With Nonviolent Communication* **by Melanie Sears, RN, MBA** • Leveraging more than 25 years nursing experience, Melanie demonstrates the profound effectiveness of NVC to create lasting, positive improvements to patient care and the health care workplace. 112pp • **$9.95**

Parenting From Your Heart: *Sharing the Gifts of Compassion, Connection, and Choice* **by Inbal Kashtan** • Filled with insight and practical skills, this booklet will help you transform your parenting to address every day challenges. 48pp • **$8.95**

Raising Children Compassionately: *Parenting the Nonviolent Communication Way* **by Marshall B. Rosenberg, Ph.D.** • Learn to create a mutually respectful, enriching family dynamic filled with heartfelt communication. 32pp • **$7.95**

The Surprising Purpose of Anger: *Beyond Anger Management: Finding the Gift* **by Marshall B. Rosenberg, Ph.D.** • Marshall shows you how to use anger to discover what you need, and then how to meet your needs in more constructive, healthy ways. 48pp • **$8.95**

Teaching Children Compassionately: *How Students and Teachers Can Succeed With Mutual Understanding* **by Marshall B. Rosenberg, Ph.D.** • In this national keynote address to Montessori educators, Marshall describes his progressive, radical approach to teaching that centers on compassionate connection. 48pp • **$8.95**

We Can Work It Out: *Resolving Conflicts Peacefully and Powerfully* **by Marshall B. Rosenberg, Ph.D.** • Practical suggestions for fostering empathic connection, genuine co-operation, and satisfying resolutions in even the most difficult situations. 32pp • **$7.95**

What's Making You Angry? *10 Steps to Transforming Anger So Everyone Wins* **by Shari Klein and Neill Gibson** • A powerful, step-by-step approach to transform anger to find healthy, mutually satisfying outcomes. 32pp • **$7.95**

Available from www.NonviolentCommunication.com, www.CNVC.org, Amazon.com and all bookstores. Distributed by IPG: 800-888-4741